Phœbe Hesketh, daughter of the pioneer radiologist
A.E. Rayner, was born in Preston in 1909 and educated at
Cheltenham Ladies' College. She married in 1931, had three
children, and for many years lived with her family in the small
Lancashire village that she wrote about in her prose books
Rivington (1972) and *Village of the Mountain Ash* (1990). During
the Second World War she worked for the *Bolton Evening
News* and she was later a freelance lecturer, poetry teacher
and journalist, producing many articles for journals and also
scripts for the BBC. She began writing poetry at an early age,
but her first book was not published until 1939; it was
followed by eleven further volumes before her Collected
Poems, *Netting the Sun*, were gathered together in 1989.
Her poetry for younger readers has been published in *A Song
of Sunlight* (1974) and in *Six of the Best* (Puffin, 1989).
Phoebe Hesketh was elected a Fellow of the Royal Society of
Literature in 1956 and a Fellow of the University of Central
Lancashire in 1990. She now lives at Heath Charnock in
Lancashire.

PHOEBE HESKETH

The Leave Train

NEW AND SELECTED POEMS

ENITHARMON PRESS LONDON 1994

ITS

ublished in the following:
y Life, *Critical Quarterly*,
ish, *The Independent*,
The Listener, New English Review, New Statesman, The Observer, Other Poetry, Outposts, Poetry Review, Punch, Rialto, The Spectator, Stand, The Sunday Times, Time and Tide, The Times Literary Supplement, Writing Women.

Acknowledgement is also due to Granada Television, and to the BBC, which has broadcast some of the poems on Radios 3 and 4, and on Radio Merseyside.

Arturo Di Stefano's painting *Montelimar* (oil on linen, 74¾ x 56¾ inches, 1992) is reproduced by kind permission of the artist, Christie's Corporate Collection and the Purdy Hicks Gallery, London.

First published in 1994
by the Enitharmon Press
36 St George's Avenue
London N7 0HD

Distributed in Europe
by Password (Books) Ltd
23 New Mount Street
Manchester M4 4DE

Distributed in the USA
by Dufour Editions Inc.
PO Box 449, Chester Springs
Pennsylvania 19425

ISBN 1 870612 54 X

Set in Bembo by Bryan Williamson, Frome
and printed in Great Britain by
The Cromwell Press, Broughton Gifford, Wiltshire

CONTENTS

By the same author

POETRY

Poems (Manchester, Sherratt and Hughes, 1939)
Lean Forward, Spring! (London, Sidgwick and Jackson, 1948)
No Time for Cowards (London, Heinemann, 1952)
Out of the Dark (London, Heinemann, 1954)
Between Wheels and Stars (London, Heinemann, 1956)
The Buttercup Children (London, Hart-Davis, 1958)
Prayer for Sun (London, Hart-Davis, 1966)
A Song of Sunlight (London, Chatto and Windus, 1974)
Preparing to Leave (London, Enitharmon, 1977)
The Eighth Day (London, Enitharmon, 1980)
A Ring of Leaves (Birmingham, Hayloft, 1985)
Over the Brook (Leicester, Taxus, 1986)
Netting the Sun (Petersfield, Enitharmon, 1989)
Sundowner (London, Enitharmon, 1992)

PROSE

My Aunt Edith (London, Peter Davies, 1966;
Preston, Carnegie, 1990)
Rivington: The Story of a Village (London, Peter Davies, 1972;
Newton Abbot, Country Book Club, 1974)
What Can the Matter Be? (Penzance, United Writers, 1985)
Rivington: Village of the Mountain Ash (Preston, Carnegie, 1990)

THE FIRST DAY

The spotted fawn
Awoke in small leaf-netted suns
Tattooing him with coins where he lay
Beside his mother's warmth the first day
That gave him light,
The day that played him tunes
In water-music washing over stones
And leaf-edged undertones,
The day he learned the feel
Of dew on grass
Cool, cool, and wet,
Of sun that steals the dew with sudden heat,
And heard the fret
In wind-turned willow leaves and wrinkled pool,
The day that filled his lungs with pollened wind
And smell of bracken, earth, and dell-deep moss,
The day he came to know
Sharp hunger and the flow
Of milk to comfort his small emptiness,
The strangeness of his legs,
The bulwark of his mother's side,
The solace of her pink tongue's first caress,
Her snow-soft belly for his sheltering,
The rhythm of his needs
For movement and for rest,
For food and warmth and nest
Of flattened grass to fold himself in sleep.

THE PANTHER AND THE ANTELOPE

Black queen treading the night,
The panther passes.
Her felted foot
Crushes the mosses as she moves
Among the rushes thronged between
Her lair and a hidden pool
Fringed with reeds and grasses.

In the pool an antelope
Kisses his darkly-mirrored lips
With mole-soft muzzle as he sips
The cool and moon-washed water.
Smooth as silk the panther slips,
A loosened shadow through the trees;
Only her hot breath on the breeze
Fans the hanging flowers.

Though unaware, the antelope
Is shivering in the languid air
For jungle-hunter knows no wrong
In plundering the innocent.
Her body knotted to a thong,
The muscled panther crouches there
With burning eyes and rhythmic tail
Measuring the seconds while
She grips him in her stare.

And though his life is in the bud
And tall-branched antlers in his head
Are acorn-small,
He will not drink the huge moon dry
In mud below the pool...
The jungle silence sharpens with his cry.
Now she, voluptuous in her bed,
Is folded in a crimson sleep
While frightened creatures watch and boldly creep
In fearful safety round her bloodied dreams.

TOM RICH

Tom Rich, the gardener,
has a strawberry mark on his face;
his hands are wide enough to span
the fattest vegetable-marrow.
With shirt-sleeves rolled,
forearm muscles swelled,
he pushes his comrade barrow to feed the roses.

In April sun he prunes each bush
deftly as a hairdresser
with skilful secateurs.
On the backs of his hands the straw-gold hairs
glint among foxy freckles.
Now he is planting out
seedlings pale from long confinement
in the potting-shed:
the crooked, cumbrous fingers
approaching with gargantuan love
take each one gently as a dove
carrying home a feather to her nest.

Slowly he weeds the border,
his large boots
moving like careful barges near the roots
of coltness gem.
His giant shadow falls
where lilliputian ferns are waving
green signals to the butterflies:
cabbage-whites on dusty wings
zig-zag away, and booming bees
dizzying in-and-out of early flowers,
drugged with laburnum showers,
mumble in nectar-drunken drone
at his approach.

A caravanning snail with silver trail
removes its home to safety at the edge
of the strong box-hedge.
But not a violet need shield its head –
this grandson of Colossus
moves carefully as a deer
picking a dry-foot way among damp mosses.

Tom with his strawberry-face is rooted
strong as a tree in the garden.
And faithful like the robin
he never deserts
when the sundial's capped with snow,
but stays around, warming his hands and his dinner
at the outhouse fire,
throwing crumbs to the birds,
sharing their patience.

LYRIC EVENING

The afternoon closed round us like a witch
Grey-haired with rain.
In the twist of misshapen thorns we saw her nature
Spiteful and dark
Bent hunchback down to brush the rocky cheek
Of crags in a withered kiss.
The harridan in rusty rags of bracken
Sat in a stone-grey huddle,
Chilled us in scarves of mist.

Then she leapt up and shrieked
Through crevices of deserted cottages –
No moss or fern could gentle that sawmill voice.
And she blocked our road gesticulating
With timber-creaking limbs until we fled
Her raw hill-weather fury.

But as we walked downhill together slowly
The evening rose to meet us like a lyric
With straight smoke from the valley,
And lights pricking their yellow stars
Through winter-roughened larches.

ST LUKE'S SUMMER

Now is the tolling time
Between the falling and the buried leaf;
A solitary bell
Saddens the soft air with the last knell
Of summer.
Gone is the swallow's flight, the curving sheaf;
The plums are bruised that hung from a bent bough,
Wasp-plundered apples in the dew-drenched grass
Lie rotting now.
Doomed with the rest, the daggered hawthorn bleeds
Bright crimson beads
For the birds' feast.
Gone are the clusters of ripe cherries,
Tart crabs, and damsons where a bullfinch tarried,
Only the camp-fire coloured rowan berries
Blaze on.
Now is the time of slow, mist-hindered dawns,
Of sun that stains
Weeds tarnished early in the chilling rains,
Of coarse-cut stubble fields
Where starlings gather, busy with the scant grain,
And with hoarse chattering proclaim
The spent season.
Now are the last days of warm sun
That fires the rusted bracken on the hill,
And mellows the deserted trees
Where the last leaves cling, sapless, shrunk, and yellow.
A robin finds some warm October bough
Recapturing his song
Of Aprils gone,
And tardy blackbirds in the late-green larch
Remember March.

TRUANT

Sing a song of sunlight
My pocket's full of sky –
Starling's egg for April
Jay's feather for July.
And here's a thorn-bush three bags full
Of drift-white wool.

They call him dunce, and yet he can discern
Each mouse-brown bird,
And call its name and whistle back its call,
And spy among the fern
Delicate movement of a furred
Fugitive creature hiding from the day.
Discovered secrets magnify his play
Into a vocation.

Laughing at education
He knows where the redshank hides her nest, perceives
A reed-patch tremble when a coot lays siege
To water territory.
Nothing escapes his eye:
A ladybird
Slides like a blood-drop down a spear of grass;
The sapphire sparkle of a dragon-fly
Redeems a waste of weeds.
Collecting acorns, telling the beads of the year
On yew tree berries, his mind's too full for speech.

Back in the classroom he can never find
Answers to dusty questions, yet could teach,
Deeper than knowledge,
Geometry of twigs
Scratched on a sunlit wall,
History in stones,
Seasons told by the fields' calendar –
Living languages of Spring and Fall.

NORTHERN STONE

Sap of the sullen moor is blood of my blood.
A whaleback ridge and whiplash of the wind
Stripping the branches in a rocking wood –
All these are of my lifestream, scoured and thinned.

Lack-leaf spring, monotonous days of wet
And grudging acres where the sheep live hard;
Unfeatured country where no weed can set
A yellow eye to light reluctant sward;
The untamed fell, spreading a matted mane,
Gold as a lion below the dying sun,
And cat-o'-nine-tails of the scourging rain
Companion me when every friend has gone.

And now the grape-bloom of a night-blue hill
Surrounds my spirit with a deep content;
O, profligate with stars, the night is still
Regenerate of all that day has spent!

Lurks no concession in this northern stone
And stubborn soil and shock-haired tufts of reed?
The few who thrive here feed upon the bone;
None look for plenty in the famished seed.

Yet, breath of my breath, they have me by the throat,
These dark, indifferent moors that take no care
For life resurgent in the starving root
And love undaunted by the hostile air.

GIRAFFES

Beyond the brassy sun-stare where each shade
Crouches beneath its substance at mid-noon
The tall giraffes are gathered in a glade
Grazing the green fruit of the midday moon.
Patched with sienna shadows of the jungle
In pencil-slender attitudes they stand
Grotesque in camouflage, each curve and angle
Merged into the backcloth of the land.

Circus creatures of a poet's dreaming,
Secure on stilts they seldom need to run,
Keeping silent watch on hunters' scheming,
Moving unseen, unheard, are swiftly gone.
Strange genesis in which the substance seeming
The shadow is the secret of the sun.

I AM NOT RESIGNED

The will forbids; the heart has flown
Down long green tunnels overgrown
By arches leafed with memory.
Here's the brushwood pile: the wood,
The log-filled waggon; here we stood
And watched it creak downhill.
Blue puddles of inverted sky,
Blue smoke, blue haze, a curlew's cry
Come back and hurt me still.

The road goes where we cannot go;
Mist hides all we long to know.
Only the black lake frets and glooms
And fills the mind's deserted rooms
With images of yesterday.

A glen of shadows, hills where rise
Legends from greener centuries,
The house beside the lake, the lane
That leads the heart back home again –
All these invade my mind.
And though the bridges, stiles and streams
Remain, we cross them in our dreams;
And *I am not resigned*.

IT WAS NOT I

There came a night I slept for hate of day,
Then followed days I feared to leave the night.
Reluctantly I faced the challenge: Light!
With shaking hands I shut the dark away:
Necessity stood naked on the brink
Of death – I clothed her hating every stitch
And longed to tread her helpless in the ditch
Where struggle dies and pride and purpose sink.

It was not I who waited on despair
Till misery became my comforter,
Or nursed paralysis to health until
I moved in spite of my reluctant will.
The motive was not mine that moulded pain
Into a cup that breaks and brims again.

WORDSWORTH'S OLD AGE

Sunlight once played upon the granite ledges
Now shadowed by austerity of mind;
And from the place where primroses have rested
The warm earth has declined.
Cold is the rock face, moss and lichen banished
To green forgotten springs locked deep below
A frozen crust; the celandine has vanished.
Where star and violet shone now falls the snow.

You, the river brimmed with life reflecting
Forms and colours we could not perceive
Until you shone the mirror through our blindness,
Are now a dry bed where the willows grieve.

Can old age answer for a poet's dying?
(Those bony fingers pinch a shrinking flame.)
Or was it passion cold upon the anvil
That failed your sensual heart till no spark came
To startle innate iron with sudden glory
Transcending vulgar metal? Was it shame
Or sanctioned love that tamed your blue-hawk spirit,
Drugging the Muse with kindness and with calm,
And dropped domestic oil on seething torrents
To soothe such ecstasy with deadly balm?

You who wrote your name in rock and rainbow
And sang of summits till you dwarfed the earth,
Are now tight-lipped, ungiving as the gritstone,
Lodge for the bones where once a bird had birth.
When the heart is out no hearth-fire warms the poet;
To find a spark his will must strike on stone.
But stone is hostile to a tired spirit –
The poet is dead: a man lives on alone.

THE MALLARD

Brown-checked, neat as new spring tweed,
A mallard, wing-stretched in the sun,
Watched from the bank of a beer-bubble stream
Her ducklings, one after one,
Daring, dipping in dazzling weed,
Nuzzling joyful mud.
Black and yellow, downy as bees,
They busied about a fringe of reed
In a paddled nursery pool.

The mother, content, lay dry,
Relaxed her wings, slackened her throat,
Dared to close one bead-black eye
When swift as terror a lightning stoat
Forked and flashed upstream.

Splatter and splash of mother and young –
Feathered drops whirled in a storm of fear,
Water thrashed in flight.
A stone for the stoat – I flung it near
And stood alone, not knowing what fate
Lay crouched in wait, while the stillness there
Grew ominous and bright.

SKELETON BRIDE

I come to you now to woo your mind
(Because your heart is dead)
Stripped of defence that you may find
New pleasures for the head
In my chaste and calcined tread.

See how my ribs let the moonlight in!
Feel the sockets of my eyes –
Each one pockets a star; I grin
For you may not chastise
Responses of the flesh, the bloom
Of shoulder, cheek, and breast;
The cramped cell of your mind has room
To give a skeleton rest
And still be unpossessed.

I come not to possess or claim
A handshake or a glance;
I come to challenge a living shame
With death's revealing dance
That flings the concealing veils aside –
All seven on the floor –
To strip me naked, heaven's bride,
Till now I stand before
Your gaze, a woman no more.

O won't you test my rigid wrist
And fingers pencil-fine?
Explore the mouth where once you kissed
Your soul away in mind?
And come and take me now dissolved
Of every warm desire –
Each curve and cave and clasping limb
Resolved in Arctic fire?

Fastidious and proud, you may
Remain in your embrace
Remarking the intricate way
My bones fit into place,
Glad that I have no face,
No force to pull your soul away
From gravity to grace.

INTEGRATION

The undertow is strong tonight, my love;
Throughout the day my harnessed forces row
Against the tide, but now the unsleeping flow
Omnipotent has swept me to your side.

My little boat, fragile among the reeds
Of circumstance, created for the needs
Of man to cross the straits of loneliness,
Is tugged two ways; and I must ride the stress
Where heart and head are crossed waves on the tide.

Face to the shore, I haul my will to land;
There is no helm that reason cannot turn.
Only the kick of a wave diverts my hand;
And a star can sting and burn.

The will must rest; and now I am ashore,
A Nothing upon a bank of sleep, whose soul
Unknowing has drifted where itself is known.

IMAGINATION

The primrose shape was printed on His mind
Before the primal dawn, before the springs
And rivers gathered from imagined rain;
Before the earth was made He knew all things.

Darkness cannot blind the eyes of light
To every creature's form, before the seed
Forests of sound and colour fill His sight;
Imagination generates the deed.

Darkly in a glass the shadows move
And in the dark we see our human race
Reflected from the archetype of Love,
And dare to dream the hidden *face to face*.

THE BUTTERCUP CHILDREN

Down the dusty lane of summer
Thick with scent, tangled with honeysuckle,
The children come so slowly
You'd think the afternoon would lie for ever
Sleeping along the hedges without shadow.

School is the past; tomorrow is only a name,
And sorrow has no share in this enchantment.
They live in the immediate delight
Of butterflies and clocks of dandelion
Blown as soon as looked at, without time
To jostle them from one thought to another.

Theirs is the present
Wide open as a daisy to the sun;
They do not bruise it in their gathering.
What though these shining buttercup bouquets
Droop in their eager hands?
The gold ungrudging petals drop behind
Uncounted through a timeless afternoon.

ON IONA

Boy and girl are picking irises
Beside the hidden stream that feeds the sea;
Their laughter is as yellow as the flowers
Among the steady green.
Inconsequent as butterflies they flit
Zig-zagging down the valley to the shore
Heedless of warning voices left behind
Like sandals on a stone.

Home is forgotten in the barefoot joy
Of running on wet sands and finding shells
Fluted, delicate as columbines,
Pinker than a baby's finger-nail.

Rock-pools reflect two giant fishermen
Gazing down with eyes grown wonder-wide
At fans of weed and floating mermaid's hair
And fringed anemones darker than wine.

With a shout the sea is calling them,
Rocketing spray and flinging on the sand
Exploding bubbles along the curving line
Of the last wave home.

HOUSE IN THE TREE

The house in the tree now tenanted by the wind
Was once your hiding-place –
Green-foot, goat-foot, you leapt above earth;
Each day I see your face
Laughing between leaves, mocking at care.

This leaning ladder beckons you again
To windy roof-tops where you found the sun.
Neither the slant rain
Nor the grey wolf-hollow wind
Could daunt your coloured escapades.

Yours was a rainbow mind
Of sudden come-and-go,
Winking through trees like water,
Vanished like the puff of a dandelion-clock.
I see you now
Gazing enraptured at the year's first snow,
Pranking through fields with a butterfly-net.

You discovered a world that was gay
With zig-zag butterflies and feathered snow,
Crack of bonfires and the polished bay
In prickly chestnuts, handkerchiefs stained red
With blackberry juice.
Days were coloured beads upon a thread
Each one brighter than the one before.

Now, no sound,
No dizzy wheels flashing, scorning the ground –
Your circus bicycle is shut away
With rust and cobwebs that you never knew.
Yet on a summer night that smells of hay
When the screeching barn-owl tears the years away
I find you again
Asleep in your tent, untouched by the prowling dark
And the difficult joy grown strong through living with pain.

THE FOX

It was twenty years ago I saw the fox
Gliding along the edge of prickling corn,
A nefarious shadow
Between the emerald field and bristling hedge
On velvet feet he went.

The wind was kind, withheld from him my scent
Till my threaded gaze unmasked him standing there
The colour of last year's beech leaves, pointed black,
Poised, uncertain, quivering nose aware
Of danger throbbing through each licking leaf.
One foot uplifted, balanced on the brink
Of perennial fear, the hunter hunted stood.

I heard no alien stir in the friendly wood,
But the fox's sculpted attitude was tense
With scenting, listening, with a seventh sense
Flaring to the alert; I heard no sound
Threaten the morning; and followed his amber stare,
But in that hair-breadth moment, that flick of the eye,
He vanished.

And now, whenever I hear the expectant cry
Of hounds on the empty air
I look to a gap in the hedge, and see him there
Filling the space with fear; the trembling leaves
Are frozen in his stillness till I hear
His leashed-up breathing – how the stretch of time
Contracts within the flash of re-creation!

BLEASDALE: THE WOODEN CIRCLE

*The Wooden Circle at Bleasdale and that at Woodhenge are believed
to be the oldest in Britain (circa 1400 B.C.). The wooden stumps from
Bleasdale, now in Preston Museum, are the only ones still in existence.*

In the sun of a late summer I return
To the land where I was born –
The true magnetic North with its dark moods
And heather-shouldered fells where the green corn
Delays the farmers' year.

Here is the stream that washed our youth away
Under the bridge's eye,
And the black unblinking pond, thick-lashed with reeds,
That gazes at but never holds the sky.

This country is dynamic, beckoning
Her sons back to the stormy solitudes
And tawny marshes where reluctant spring
Retards the leaf; vitality unspent
Is leashed within the acorn and the bud.
And in these brooding silences between
Age-twisted oaks and bristled firs there breathes
A spirit older than the ageless earth.

A shawl of sun surrounds the infant church
That of itself can give back merely shadows
From stones that gave it birth.
But the soul of man was born when he stood up
From dust to gaze in wonder at the sun.
After the seedless silences of cold
He looked to the east and saw his golden god
Risen from nowhere to subdue the night.

Time falls away; unmeasured ages wheel
Through ice and stone and bronze till now we stand
On the circle where our fathers sang to the sun.

Here priest and peasant have stood
In the first prayer facing towards the east.
And wonder, ever young, still gropes behind
The sun for motive, feels the muscled wind
And questions whence it came.

RECAPITULATION

Whenever I return
Anchorless to that harbour
Where the grey houses in the grey rain
And the poppy-coloured boat out in the bay
Are branded on my brain, I meet you on the quay –
In the tea-shop with its windows to the sea
Framed in a foam of lace.

Through the mist and the half-sun
Dropping on golden gardens and the bronze
Bitter chrysanthemums,
Again I see your face.

And while my unaware companion
Babbles of boats and birds,
I'm caught away from words; the holiday place
Escapes me in my errant capturing
Of thoughts on wing, a mood that backs away,
A form, half-shadow – how a slant of light
Plays on these known surroundings like a tune
That recapitulates.

RECLAIMED

A fallen star
Cooled from the sun to the brink of death we are
Till Love awakes and warms us into life.

Stiffened waves relax and curl around
Untrodden shores, exploring empty caves;
Fish flicker into life and flash upstream;
The long grey dream
In stony river-beds is broken by
Water thrashing down a mountain-side.
A rigid forest stirs towards the sun,
Lets forth its birds like some old falconer
Forgetful of his art
Till memory informs his frozen brain
That Pan is here; the world is green; and all
The ache of living – beauty spiked with pain –
Begins again.

Branches cradling the wind
Shake out pink-fisted blossom; crumpled leaves
Expanding in the light unclose
The blue forget-me-not, the first wild rose
Pale as a shell from centuries of cold.
And man and woman, gazing upon these,
Rejoice in freedom of the hills and seas
But by their need for love themselves are bound;
And each surrenders wholly to the other.

Such union cannot hold;
Not only trees but lovers must grow old
And die.
Fear creeps around them; Death comes near to try
Their wholeness with his dark dividing rod –
And there's no hiding-place from his huge eye.
Like drowning men they reach out for a god
Imploring him to listen and to save.

There is no shelter in the toppling wave,
No warmth in the opening cave,
No consolation in the thought of Truth,
Goodness and Beauty without human form.
Only a man can understand their need
And serve them as a god.
Pan with his goat-legs has escaped, and fills
The air with wordless echoes and a sound
Of laughter that intensifies the wound
Of separation.

Only a man, mortal as ourselves,
Wearing our clothes, sharing our daily food
Can clear the brambled path for our return.
A carpenter drives nails into the wood
Towards the day when gathering beads of blood
Shall shine like rowan-berries from his wrists.
But now the footpath twists
From light to dark, and truth half-understood
Fades from the desperate mind; the unguarded heart
Cries out in terror at its loneliness.
A mist comes down and all is blind again.

Where is the promised moment of return
To more than Eden when we played half-grown
Like children in the sun?
We've searched the planets, lost ourselves to find
Our faces in the mirror staring back
The eternal question that has no reply.

A fallen star
Cooled from the sun to the brink of death we are
Till Love awakes and leads us into life.

LOVE WITHOUT FRONTIERS

To have met you and loved you and not to have stayed
Till footsteps dragged and lark-music delayed
Its ascension,
To have left on the up-beat and not to have known
The end of surprise,
To have kissed and departed and wept and grown wise
In knowledge of love – by this we are made
Immortal, inviolate: none can invade
A love without frontiers that sees without eyes,
Is present in absence and never denies
The unexplored country beyond.

EVERGREEN

The language of life is green
And in this tongue I send you messages.
Although we may not meet, the way between
Is leafed with words; meaning unfolds and grows
Through white and leafless silences that lie
Bare as the Winter of expectancy.
Not dead but sleeping – this much knowledge knows:
Hope is an evergreen that dare not die.

THE VINE

All my fruit is yours for you are mine,
The root and stem from which my tendrils twine;
You are the warmth that swells my tender grapes.

My leaves are hands uplifted to your light;
Each palm grows bright to catch the falling sun.
And when the waiting nets of night
Are wide to hold earth's ripeness we are one –
Root, branch, and leaf and rounding fruit begun
In life's full circle.

White root, go deep
That in your tunnelled darkness I may sleep;
Strong branch, reach high
Till my green hands, glad servers of the sun,
Receive the cup of water and of fire
And find it brimmed with wine –
I drink you, drain you till my life in yours
Is yours in mine.

PRAYER FOR SUN

Two trees outside my window stood;
I might have lived in the middle of a wood
For all I saw of the sun – the light
Flowed into a rowan's beaded head
To glaze the berries paint-box red
Or raise new blossom whiter than bread,
But the sun was hidden from sight.

Leaf-locked with the rowan a whitebeam pressed
Against my window; blinded the west;
Scratched the pane when I lay there ill;
Trickled with rain down my window-sill.
Visitors said: 'What a friendly tree!'
Of my faithful enemy.
At Candlemas, down on my knees,
I begged the landlord to fell the trees:
'One drinks the morning light away;
One drains the evening dregs. Midday,
Midnight are laced in grave-green gloom.
I must have the sun in my room!'

The landlord laughed; his bowler-hat
Was as hard as his look; his answer flat
As a paving-stone: 'I must have rain.
Trees attract it. Don't ask again,
Remember you live on a watershed
By courtesy,' he curtly said.

I watched the trees grow big with dark,
Opened the window, touched each bark –
Whitebeam with left hand, rowan with right,
And prayed for light.

I lay in my leaf-green grave again;
Two trees grew tall behind my brain,
Darkened my dreams with leaves and rain.
Lost in a house in a wood I wept:
'Lord, pluck this whitebeam from my eye,
This rowan that blocks the morning sky.'
I heard the thunder of God's reply,
Yet still I slept –
'Gather their branches one by one;
Twist their roots – if rain or sun
May ever by prayer be won!'

I woke. The visiting day was white
As a stranger stripped before me: Light.
I zipped the curtains back; the sky
Dazzled the window, drew my eye
From where it sought to where it found
A light-flash later – on the ground.

Was I awake or rocked in dream?
With leaves hair-locked in the garden gate,
Below me shivered the tough whitebeam
Felled by the axe of Fate.
One pang was drowned in murderous joy –
Whose was the hand strong to destroy
This more-than-human tree?
The storm was God's but it broke through me.

The landlord swore at God's will done
In a tree that wrestled the wind and won
My case for the sun.
Alone, the rowan tapped window and wall
Tossing its sun-embroidered shawl
On the empty air
Till the camp-fire coloured beads burned down
And emerald leaves shrank nutmeg-brown
From branches skeleton-bare.

Like bones they rattled the wind and cold,
Grew black as I grew bold
To summon the landlord once again:
'Your rowan will bring down no more rain!'

They called me a witch; dragged it away;
Carted the rowan, bald and grey,
Tossed me a twig for the evil done
And left me to live – and die – with the sun.

CATS

Cats are contradictions: tooth and claw
Velvet-padded;
Snowflake-gentle paw
A fist of pins;
Kettles on the purr
Ready to spit;
Black silk then bristled fur.

Cats are of the East –
Scimitar and sphinx;
Sunlight striped with shade.
Leopard, lion, lynx
Moss-footed in a frightened glade;
Slit eyes an amber glint
Or boring through the darkness cool as jade.

Cats have come to rest
Upon the cushioned West.
Here, dyed-in-the-silk,
They lap up bottled milk
But must return
To the mottled woods of spring
Making the trees afraid
With leaf and wing
A-flutter at the movement in the fern.

Midnight-wild with phosphorescent eyes
Cats are morning-wise
Sleeping as they stare into the sun,
Blind to the light,
Deaf to echoing cries
From a ravaged wood;
Cats are black and white rolled into one.

FISHERMAN POET

(for Herbert Palmer)

He was farouche
with grey moustache,
an otter's look in his wild brown eyes
as he hooked a trout;
a wolf's snarl in his anger
flaring for a fight.

Yet he loved his adversary,
scourging weather;
chose to fish upstream;
unswerving will
followed the curving river to its source
in bed of rock,
bristle of heather.

There he mocked
flat, felted poets;
dim, grey speech down-toned
to pavements made him howl.

When no one listened
he sang to the wind – loud
songs till the larches bowed.
He cried to the stars,
nailed his meaning to the mast
of the tallest pine in the forest.

The stars opened their ears;
the wind's thong lashed;
but no one hears
his true song
now the wind has lain down
with otter and wolf,
and the poet on an island of reeds
returns to himself.

DEATH OF A GARDENER

He rested through the winter, watched the rain
On his cold garden, slept, awoke to snow
Padding the window, thatching the roof again
With silence. He was grateful for the slow
Nights and undemanding days; the dark
Protected him; the pause grew big with cold.
Mice in the shed scuffled like leaves; a spark
Hissed from his pipe as he dreamed beside the fire.

All at once light sharpened; earth drew breath,
Stirred; and he woke to strangeness that was spring,
Stood on the grass, felt movement underneath
Like a child in the womb; hope troubled him to bring
Barrow and spade once more to the waiting soil.
Slower his lift and thrust; a blackbird filled
Long intervals with song; a worm could coil
To safety underneath the hesitant blade.
Hands tremulous as cherry branches kept
Faith with struggling seedlings till the earth
Kept faith with him, claimed him as he slept
Cold in the sun beside his upright spade.

DILEMMA

As he lay dead,
frost-blue eyes hooded,
he looked like a Viking chieftain.
Grey-headed with strength and wisdom,
he needed no helmet or sword –
centuries slumbered in his folded arms.

They robed him in white;
and we were silent in his presence
listening for commands.
When fire had transformed
oakwood, roses, flesh, to ashes
we held the casket bewildered.
He had two wives;
and the dead wife was our mother;
but the widow cried, 'Scatter
them in the wood where he met me!'

Under the oaks, sowing, we paused,
dust on our hands:
'Let us divide him
as life divided him...'
So we emptied half on our mother's grave.
And no voice came from the yew tree
to question and condemn.

HE SAVED OTHERS...

(for A.E. Rayner, Pioneer in Radiology)

He's in the dark-room again
reaching up with schoolboy elation
to examine the dripping plates –
ribs, femur, pelvis.
Here's a beautiful gall-stone
sharp against shadow,
and this obscene bud
swelling in the honeycomb cells.

Faithfully the reel unwinds; he looks
into himself
having nurtured for years the avaricious flower
expanding in his entrails,
thrusting roots and petals through a vital part.

Without hope from the start
they tied up the bowel, made
makeshift with his guts,
massaged his heart,
fed him oxygen and blood.

From his hot white tent
he peers at us faraway children, struggles to reach
out and save, but the rope of speech
frays in twitching fingers.
He slips back into a whispering valley,
groping for a ledge of comfort.

Plucking the bedclothes, suddenly he jerks his head,
clutches iron rails from a gulley of pain,
scrabbles for a handhold, a jutting rock
on which to belay his life.

He was always a mountaineer – not for fame
but to test and find himself.
To younger men he is a challenge, a name,
but to us the roof
wrenched from our built-up world.

47

SALLY

She was a dog-rose kind of girl:
Elusive, scattery as petals;
Scratchy sometimes, tripping you like briars.
She teased the boys
Turning this way and that, not to be tamed
Or taught any more than the wind.
Even in school the word 'ought' had no meaning
For Sally. On dull days
She'd sit quiet as a mole at her desk
Delving in thought.
But when the sun called
She was gone, running the blue day down
Till the warm hedgerows prickled the dusk
And moths flickered out.

Her mother scolded; Dad
Gave her the hazel switch,
Said her head was stuffed with feathers
And a starling tongue.
But they couldn't take the shine out of her;
Even when it rained
You felt the sun saved under her skin.
She'd a way of escape
Laughing at you from the bright end of a tunnel,
Leaving you in the dark.

HEAT-WAVE

Heat over all; not a lark can rise
Into the arching sun;
The moor like a lion sleeping lies –
Rough mane on burning stone.
Not a harebell shakes; the wild blue flags
Of wind are folded up.
Here on the hill the air is still
As water in a cup.

DEAD BLACKBIRD

The blackbird used to come each day
listening, head sideways, for movement under the lawn,
stabbing his yellow-as-crocus bill
precisely in,
pulling out a pink elastic worm.

In winter with flirted tail
he landed on the sill for crumbs
ousting sparrows, blue-tits – even robins.
Soot-black, sleek,
his plumage shone like a dark man's head.

But this morning I looked out of the window
and saw him dead –
a crumpled bunch of feathers
rocking in the wind.

I have never seen anything dead
except flies
and stuffed animals in museums
where they make them look alive.
Dead people are hidden away
tidied into boxes,
covered with flowers.
The living talk about the dead in low voices.
Is death so ugly, uncomfortable
that people are afraid?

I am much more afraid of what I cannot see.
But I can see the blackbird;
and I know these crumpled feathers
are only rags of him, not he
with his crocus-yellow bill.

WARD F4

There is no weather in my room,
a white cube, bare
except for a bedside chest, one chair.
The window behind my bed
looks blind on a blind wall,
but I cannot turn my head.

No sky; no sun;
one lamp with hard green shade
is my daylight
and nightlight.
(No flowers, please; nowhere
to put them but on the floor.)
I face the brown door, stare
at the black knob, waiting...

Nurses come and go
brisk, kind under crackling starch.
They give me pills, injections
with cheerful remarks about the weather.
But there is no weather in my room.

For twelve months I have not seen a tree
or a patch of grass.
I think I could walk again
if I saw grass.
I shut my eyes;
I can see more with my eyes shut –
heather, a bright stream,
the flash of a bird.

Autumn, winter have wasted away;
today is the first day of spring;
and nurse says the sun is shining...

My splints are off;
my limbs feel supple
and I'm running over grass
where the willow lets down her yellow hair.

Toffee-brown chestnut buds unclose
fingers soft as silver-fox.
There's movement among branches: a speckled thrush
swings and sings, frilling the needled larch
with promised green.
Blossom and cloud pile high, higher as I pass.
I am free; the grass is warm,
yielding to my feet...

The door opens and the doctor comes in
returning me to the white cube.
He talks of tests and treatment,
makes no promises.
Improvement is slow.
Visitors come and go
bringing rain on their coats
or a bunch of flowers –
only they bring the weather into my room.

THE HORSES

Between waking and sleep
I am alone in a bright field
drifting towards a closing gate.
The gap narrows and I reach for the latch
but the black stallion arches through
trampling pale hems of dreams.
Nostrils, eyes sparking the darkness,
he is rubbed ebony at my thighs
lifting me along where I dare not go.

I left his bridle in daylight;
without reins I
melt in his muscled stride
across unseen land: no root or stone
hindering flight,
no turn for home in this curving ride.
Did we leap the gate
landing safe on the far side
with will absolved from need to fight
the dazzling dark?

Time broke with a blackbird singing
sharp as a star
nailing truth home.
It was a journey of splintered hooves
and black miles back to the field
and the white mare waiting at the gate
in first light.

BULL ALONE

Black bull, square and strong,
Foursquare against the weather,
Steams gently after rain –
Bull-vapour spiralling gently into the hawthorn.
But he's young, ready to trample storms;
His meekness breaks under the hedge.
Stretching his neck he bellows the morning out,
Trots to the gate barred
Against acquiescent heifers,
Roars over it his rage and grief,
Rubs his sorrow along the top bar
Then stands waiting
Like an uncoupled engine, new but redundant.

Alone in a field wide for cavorting
Among plentiful grass, unlaboured time,
He is sad as a caged lion,
Energy dripping to waste,
Triangular, rubbery tongue
Mournfully licking his nostrils.

Away up in a gleam of blue
A lark is threading ascending beads of song
Above five warm eggs in the grass.
The bull's ears turn, but his senses are raw
With angry suffering smelted in the blood
Felt, not understood.

RISE...

Summer lies thick along the hedgerows
foaming with chervil
splitting pods and spilling seeds
knees up in the grass, roses in her hair –
fertility act without statistics
or morals, buttons or zips
hindering fulfilment.

Alone for the first time
I walk among summer's exuberance
shoes pollen-dusted
idly scattering rusty sorrel beads
in concert with the season.
June's hot hand in mine
I swish through plumy meadows to the water
watch moor-hens' bawdy sport among the reeds
where the lake flaps content.
A trout lies shallow, frilling fins and tail;
two butterflies still damp from birth
flicker in heat of a first and last day.
And the warm rise of summer
sweats under my skin.

AND FALL

Why am I sad?
It is autumn;
leaves fall;
sun reddens early behind the hill.

Somewhere I hear
lifts going down,
lights clicking on
and feet hurrying home like leaves.

I GIVE DEATH TO A SON

Rhythmic pincer-jaws clench
and widen – the world explodes –
I give death to a son.
Tearing apart the veil he comes
protected fish from dark pool.
I push him over the weir,
land him on dry stones.

Was he anything, anywhere
behind, beyond
out there in nothingness?
Is he nothing, made aware
of cold, hunger, nakedness?

Trailing glory and slime
he is washed and dried,
grave-clothes ready warmed
by the fireside.

BOY DROWNING

Drowning is pushing through
a barrier like birth
only the elements are exchanged:
air for water.
Then, water for air,
my lungs
folded flat as butterflies' wings
struggled to expand
in a round scream.

Now I make no sound –
or they don't hear
water damming my ear-
drums, nostrils, eyes –
I fight like a salmon on grass
choked with a bubble.
I cannot rise
a third time.

CROSS

He was thorn
pierced through my flesh,
twisting away from earth's pull,
planets' rhythm.
In twitching limbs
dance was contorted;
speech leered from his mouth,
salivating words.

Hourly he beat me
with compassion's knobbed stick;
I swallowed resentment
like hairs.
My cupped hands
spilled pity's grit-in-the-eye.

Now he is gone
respite I longed for
sours the tongue.
Silence accuses;
peace whispered through grasses
dies on the wind.
Huge emptiness
engulfs my stand.
He was the cross
I leaned my life upon.

DIFFERENT

Even at school he was different,
unblemished by the usual crudities,
suffering the form bully without condemning,
turning the right cheek
when the maths master slashed his left.

The boys, unbuttoning, taunted him:
Blessed are the pure in heart!
and punched him where it hurt.
He walked alone
searching hedgerows for birds' nests,
never taking the eggs till they jeered,
hid his cap, inked his face and legs
earning him a thrashing.

Dreaming of a moorland farm
and sheep grey as native boulders
he was sent to work in the mill.
Under that chimney's dominant finger
he companioned the spinners
sharing their bread and their hunger.

Management exploited the 'Peacemaker'
confronting him with angry customers,
snags in the yarn, redundancies:
sacking comrades, they agreed with stroking voices,
was his pigeon – or dove.

Stretched like elastic beyond its give,
he was used by all, scooped out
till he seemed less than a man,
his cross hollow as a rattle.
So they called an extraordinary private meeting,
thanked him, shook him by the hand
and sent him home with a silver tray.

WALKING AWAY

Last night he walked out on himself
along the wet quay, leaving his skin behind.
The wind had no teeth for him;
the dark could not blind.

No plunge now in snake-black river-shine;
Jesus-feet carry him over
away from sad drunks slumped on benches,
and a woman's whine.

No doors locked; the world swings open
at the 'No-Entry' sign.
Through curtains he sees without envy
lovers entangled supple in sleep,
and those single figures
stiffening, drying, he fears no longer
since he walked out on himself.

REFLECTIONS

I

The great screw-turner knows
how far to turn
the thread to a hair –
hair-breadth to freedom –
but the thread holds.
One more turn
and I eat air.
Instead I choke
not dead but driven head-deep
into dead wood.

II

I am very small
and must become smaller
crowding myself out
in others' needs
till there is no I
taking up space in the cage.

III

She is untouched
growing flesh like snow
on sapling birch.
But rounding under the cold
Spring has begun
the slow, inevitable
change.
Blood, like snow, will run
urgent, purposeful, quick
under the sun.

IV
I am hollow
sucked at, squeezed by insistent ivy;
suckers have drained the sap
from live wood into gloss –
the ivy is all gloss and green-webbed hands
waving over my farewell,
coiling, clinging
twisting itself into a green tower,
quivering around my life.

'Look,' people say,
'The beautiful ivy –
how it thrives winter and summer
triumphing green
over that broken tree.'

THE METHS MEN

*Close to Strangeways Prison in Nightingale
Street, Manchester, you may see, any time you
pass, a group of destitute men just sitting there,
drinking their lives away in surgical spirit.*

(*Extract from* The Listener)

A short spit from Strangeways
the Meths Men
huddle together in Nightingale Street.
Rejects among rubble and rosebay
they're doing time
escaping from themselves
drinking day into night into day.

Behind chimneys the moon's cold eye
stares down; they don't look up
except with eyes shut,
bottle lifted in dummy comfort.

In winter
spit freezes; they shuffle
into the Hostel of the Morning Star.
Last Christmas one chap wouldn't budge,
next day couldn't –
hair frozen to ground.
He was only half-dead
so they took him to hospital
and made him half-alive.

Immortality is a long word
and surgical spirit is slow.
Here is no fox's life, red to the death.
In Nightingale Street
dust creeps into mouths and minds.
They die grey.

CHRISTMAS BLACKMAIL

Like early snow they come –
spirits of advent
through letter-box and door –
a sort of blackmail
in these dumb appeals.
How shall we choose
between the blind, lame, deaf and those
hungry eyes of children hammering
our hearts till nails
are driven through?

Confused, we turn to go, assailed
by other cries:
Save the Whale, Gorilla, Kangaroo!

GONE AWAY

When we thought him near
he was away
far side of the hill.
While in thickets we tore him apart,
ate him alive, flung his heart to the dogs,
he eluded us still.

Gone-away fox –
no hounds will bring him back;
melted in distance he runs
through Sirius, Orion.
The hungry pack
trails him in vain; suns
have gone down on his blood.

His breath is autumn mist;
yellowing leaves
glint with his topaz look.
Gone away, away, away –
he is over the brook.

I CANNOT LOOK INTO THE SUN

In your green anorak
flickering between the trees
I see you, gentle hob-nailed ghost,
a sack of logs on your back
bending towards the sunset.

In truth, I am the ghost
searching under a pile of summer
for a buried axe.

Everything was lost those last days
when we lost each other –
I tried to hold you back in the dark wood
but a blackbird sang in your head
songs I never understood
whistling you away from clocks and signposts
up a path I could not follow.

Came Autumn with binding brambles
and blinding leaves
mocking map and compass.
When winter divided us
I opened the book of rules
and heard Spring laughing at the lych-gate
where shadows change hands with light.

Can you see me wintering in the dark?
I cannot look into the sun.

BRIEF ENCOUNTER

No flowers, please, in plastic hoods –
This will not happen again;
Death's dark angel briefly broods
Indifferent to the rain

And briefly opens velvet wings
Upon the final scene
To fold them in the nick of time –
The coffin glides between.

A clockwork requiem fades out;
We rise up from our knees
Bewildered, and can almost hear
A whispered: *Next one, please.*

The 'crem' conveyor-belt slides on
From this world to the next
And everlasting spring and sun
According to the text.

O, fire, is this thy victory –
Eternal sun and spring
And truth reduced so tactfully
That Death has lost his sting?

PREPARING TO LEAVE

Attics cleared; shelves and drawers emptied;
Love-letters burned and memory purged,
I knew we had always been
Preparing to leave.
Those wedding-groups, snaps of childhood,
Babyhood, parents – back, back
To the unremembered, thrust
Deep into the dustbin.
The lid clashes louder than the Bible
That life is grass;
Possessions rust;
And man a moment of hope
From centuries' dust.

I walk out into wet fields of spring;
Plovers are circling,
Crying to the rain and the trees,
Calling their young from empty nests –
Even these
Are pulled away on the swirl and heave
Of the wind.
All things that live are preparing to leave.

MARY

Mary under the hawthorn
sat waiting
listening
watching worlds outside her ring of leaves
flying feet folded as birds
hands holding stillness.

Shadows shrank into her green tent
bunched under noonday sun.
Not a leaf, not a wing brushed the air
and the rushing world grew still as an egg –
only Mary of the cupped hands
heard the song under the shell.

CALL OF THE NORTH

We rebuilt our childhood, leaf by leaf,
that bright day snatched from summers half-forgotten
half-remembered –
the Brock running brown under bridges,
the badger at home
and a dipper with golf-ball breast
bobbing on glistening stone.

We followed the river
up lost paths, over gates and stiles
broken by the years,
past the farm whose cherry in spring
was white as their Lancashire cheese
to Delph crossroads where the beagles met.

Here Bleasdale, damson-blue, bristled with heather,
sweeps north
from the slow slope of Fairsnape taking the sun,
ageless as wind and stone.

This country calls us back by roots
deeper than oak and birch,
darker than blood
to a land of belonging.
And always the river
that washed our youth away
runs on and runs forever.

LETTER TO VINCENT

You never painted this picture, Vincent –
sunflowers pressed white on window-glass
by fingers of ice
beyond summer skills of brush and knife.
No blood in these petals
shrinking under the sun.
No gold for our looking,
only evidence of cold, unhuman magic
that even you,
painter of poems without words,
have no colours for.

WINTER DAFFODILS

Not on my knees praising God
but gazing at daffodils
brought here this winter day
by hands full of hope as greenhouses.

Their silent bugles
quicken the room with spring
unloosing knots
tightened by the driver at my back.

They wait for me
holding out the sun like a gold watch
against the shortest day
telling time that's never early
never late.

AT FOUR A.M.

In the nowhere between dark and dawn
a blackbird chips the silence
as once it chipped the shell
between darkness and light.
And I, adrift from myself
in homeless seas,
struggle towards an island
when a bird-note splinters in song
filling my hands with leaves.

MORE THAN GRASS

The crashed Messerschmidt 109 of German fighter-pilot Lieutenant Werner Knittel was found in a field near Hythe. His remains were still in the cockpit, and his identity disc gave the number from which German officials were able to identify him thirty years later.
Newspaper report 1973

In the cockpit they found his rotted tunic –
obscene fungus feeding on decay;
fields away his flung helmet
wrenched from the skull
nose and eyeholes sprouting grass.

The twisted plane, weed-pinioned,
rust-medallioned,
witnessed wind and rain wiping out death,
strumming conflict's tune into silence.

Fiddling on enemy bones
they searched for buried music
among steel and nettles:

All flesh is as grass . . .
and the grass withereth.
But the Word of the Lord endureth for ever.

They found the Word:
B 65178
engraved on a metal disc.

TRAITOR

Who says time heals forgets to add
that time destroys –
cure for agonies and griefs
is cure for joys.

Time mocks a lifelong loyalty
by stretching out to prove
how death's unanswering certainty
hollows the heart of love.

The lover bereft who swore to die
still lives through time's blank gaze
that stares him out while years trudge by
through stony nights and days.

When fond recapturings escape
memory's unguarded nets
mind alone works on to shape
what heart forgets.

Time's a traitor, subtle, slow
to change with twist and crack
our needs – if loved ones could return
we would not wish them back.

JOURNEY

I have died many times –
every night and every morning when
I leave the unknown darkness
where most I am alive
seeing shapes and colours never seen by day.

I died with my mother and my father –
and the roof was blown off my world.

Summers and winters drifted by
till the snow was a white cherry
shaken outside my window.
A blackbird whistled the world awake
and my son to be born in autumn
quickened as I stepped on the first daisies.

There was singing in the sap
that ended in his green death
playing by the river.
Then I was hollow as a wren's egg
blown by a schoolboy,
coming to life only in the green darkness
where his tent was pitched
under the willow.

One night he took my hand
telling of my journey over land and water
beginning again,
and he spoke to my daughter before birth.

Again the cherry and the blackbird,
falling leaf and snow
in magic circles
till she grew out of me –
more surely than being born –
when I'd grown into her,
made her life my own.

For that I had to suffer
a hard season of no growth
pruned low below the sunrise.
But life holds, draws, pulls
after light has gone
till the hidden flower opens
reaching for the sun.

SECOND CHILDHOOD

Free as a thistle, white hair blowing,
he wanders through fields
leaving gates open as he leaves doors at home.
Without direction his days are slanted
by shadow and sun
easy as a weathercock swinging
on the wind's heel.
Pulling sorrel seeds through finger and thumb
he scatters the coral beads,
tramples buttercups to gold-dust on his boots.

High time is harvest; a bronze moon
hangs over the hill;
by day the sun
ripens slowly as red fruit.
Wading through sand-coloured corn,
he snatches the prawn-whiskered barley
to play with all winter.

Cuckoo! Cuckoo! Grass-blade to mouth
he answers the bodiless voice,
wonder-gazing into the wide blue
bowl of infinity.

Happy, happy – this childhood is surer
than a child's,
unthreatened, outlasting life.

WHAT IS A PERSON?

Pull the rose apart –
corolla, stamens, calyx
analyse and count –
rose and scent are gone.

X-ray the patient's head;
explore the brain;
explain nerve-centres dead.
Take him in for life.

On Ward C3
they sit and stare and sleep;
from stonewall faces looking out
they do not see.

Only the new admission's a misfit
groping his way back from sterile corridors
to loved, familiar rooms,
fumbling the key
while words he needs
scatter like birds from the top of his head.

Passport missing, this refugee
stumbles past a nurse into the garden
and finds himself at home.
The roses speak for him
smoothing away confusion.
Stuffing his emptied pockets with dead heads
he discusses varieties with the gardener
having more knowledge than he
who mistakes him for the new doctor.

A nurse steers him in to tea
among patients slopping food,
grimacing backward into apehood.
And a shutter slams across him
half-man, half-wood, cruelly aware
of sunlight and roses in a lost garden.

WHAT IS GOD?

I have not seen God face to face –
how can I love Him
whose answers to my questions are
silences in stone and star,
whose presence is my loneliness?

Incomprehensible Three-in-One,
how can I love Thee,
One-in-Three?

I love ordinary people
touchable, fallible
speaking my own tongue.

I love the real sun
whose warmth I feel
in whose light I live.
I love the green sap rising
from darkness into apple,
ape and man
becoming breath, mind, spirit –
invisible, intangible
three in one.
I love the mystery
that has no name.

I AM

Considering stars,
sand-grains, shells –
spiralling infinities –
I am nothing,
uncounted as pebbles,
sparrows, grass,
dispensable as one sperm
in a universe.

Among days, seasons, light-years
where is my date?
On stone washed over and over
by rivers gone under
centuries' bridges.

And I am all –
universe,
unknowable source.
Does not the sun
shine upon me?
A tree give its shelter
and a lover
identity?

WALLED IN

When closer than breathing
we stare into the gap
that is his face,
ignore the hand outstretched,
where are we?

The small child
blowing a dandelion clock,
the boy with his hand in a dunnock's nest,
are nearer the answer.

Questioning, discovering worlds
whose reflection shines in them,
they know before books are opened
they came unwritten as rings
in a trout-pool,
untaught as the flow of rivers
before first rainfall.

We've grown too tall to enter
their door through the wall of our measured garden.

INVITATION

It was the smoke, blue
from hazel wood that drew us to him
raking old memories
in garnished twigs, turning
the red side under
with culinary care.

Shaken from dreams of her,
he smiled through glass dividing us.
We shared the feast to the last
flake, smoke dawdling,
a vanished presence.

Sustained, he led us through
his frozen garden.
Hang-head snowdrops
trembled under hedges,
weak from shouldering earth.
Aconites barely alight
outshone the cold.
And as we turned to go
the blue finger
of a single crocus held us
lingering
in the warmth of invitation.

VIOLET AT NINETY

Descendants stretching beyond her reach –
diminishing pearls on a string –
have long since forgotten her age.
She is pre-history, unreckoned,
head a honeycomb of cells,
some lighted, some shuttered.
When she tells of the Boer War, suffragettes,
horse-trams and buns for a farthing,
they smile indulgent disbelief.

The hungry generations tread on her dreams
knocking on the door in the wrong order.
She sees everything upside down
or in reverse –
clocks cross hands, confusing
minutes with hours as friends drop out
from her shrinking world of musical chairs.

New tides of disorder
wash over her; she remains
a rock in the river unmoved
by the changing climate; an antique fountain
in the city centre.

When a great-great-grandson
old in wisdom, whispers
the secret of happiness in her good ear,
she smiles, suddenly young,
stepping on to uncut grass from her curtained room.

WIDOWHOOD

After thirteen years
nothing is changed except
the years like birds
have printed my face with their feet
and my side of the bed
is hollow.
I've tunnelled a path from myself
to the world
but summer weeds choke it, and snow,
and my warm-handled shovel is thin
as the song of an autumn robin.

SINGLE FOOTPRINTS

Saturday night outsider
looking in through lighted windows –
families round television,
couples on sofas, children playing,
sharing worlds.

Sunday morning a closed shell;
blind windows staring;
isolation
as lepers' at squint-holes.

And Christmas, spiked with holly, tinsel,
twittering fairy-lights and mistletoe
unkissed under; making parcels
with no one's finger
on the knot that holds the bow,
Christmas
is single footprints in the snow.

YEW TREE GUEST HOUSE

In guest-house lounges
elderly ladies shrivel away
wearing bright bangles, beads, jumpers
to colour the waiting day
between breakfast and bed.

Grey widows whose beds and meals are made,
husbands tidied with the emptied cupboards,
live in mortgaged time
disguising inconsequence
with shavings of surface talk, letters
to nieces, stitches dropped in the quick-knit jacket,
picked up for makeweight meaning.

Weekdays are patterned by meals –
sole chance for speculation:
will it be cabbage or peas, boiled fish or fried?
Dead Sunday is dedicated to roast beef –
knives and forks are grips upon existence.
This diversion lengthens the journey;
and since Mrs Porter ceased to come downstairs,
ceased altogether,
the ladies at the Yew Tree Guest-House
bend more intently over their soup and sago,
draw closer to the table.

WAITING

Driftwood I have become,
flotsam divided by rocks
between two elements – once
caught in a whirlpool I spun for days
between the dream and its fading.

Now at the world's edge I sit waiting
for the wind to turn –
the grey wind rasping through marram
that has pinned me to sand.
Even the tamarisks have withdrawn
and the sea-holly and evening primrose
that loved the shore.

Sometimes a wisp of hair, sometimes a hand
waving above a wave beckons me on
where I must go to be reborn,
where driftwood knits into flower with maidenhair.

THE TUNNEL

They are dragging me back
through a bruising tunnel
from my pool of light and water –
landed fish gasping.

Do they hope to hold me there
with drips, transfusions, drugs
force-fed on air
in a blind white world of masks?

They fix me with needles,
tighten the knots
till I shrink back into myself
small enough to slip through
on the smooth, dark, narrow slide
to my pool of water and light
floating in no more pain.

Ice-fingers on my wrist
melt in summer's breath;
voices drone round a hive
brimmed with honey they would steal back.

I fight against detention
in a nowhere of stunned awakenings,
cavernous sleep
and prolonged sentence in half-light
where they cannot read the hour
or hear my clock strike.

OWL

The owl's a clock-face without fingers,
two keyholes for seeing,
striking silent as frost.

Soft, unexpected as snow,
its flight a wash
through trees without flicker of leaf,
a pocket of air
bulging with warm swallowed blood.

Out there the wood grown stiller
than winter with spring breathing blue-
bells and fern under cover;
each feather pinned; fur and whisker
twitching in windless night.
And Time flying white from the clock-tower
screeching the hour of death.

ANALYST

Not content with eyes
for the flower, he uses
tweezers, pulling stamens,
stigma, style and ovary,
bruising
the petals apart, searching
what is no longer there.

He has probed too many entries
examining hair, labia
with curious torch
that loses what it lights, provides
inadequate notes.

Somehow he must secrete
communion bread under his tongue
for the microscope.

A VERY SMALL CASUALTY

Flower
lovingly pressed in an album
petals preserved cruciform
colours dried to a moth's wing.

Rabbit
equally flat on tarmac
stamped to a flash of crimson fringed
with skin and hair
parchment-thin under tear and tread.

At human pace I see
spun from the flattened centre
the white scut blown as thistledown
and gleaming jewel-bright, upturned
to the blind indifferent world,
a single eye.

CREDO

I believe in Nothing.

And what is Nothing?
The space within you
where God is,
space between friend and friend,
star and star.
Silence of snowfall
and loved ones' absence.

What am I?

A little boat
grappling with angry waves
to keep afloat.
Driven
helpless from shore to shore,
at home only
in the wrench and roar
of waves I defy
that would wrap me in stillness
under storm, under sky
where no winds blow.

I must walk gently
as on a tightrope
now my cup is full,
must balance on air
like a kestrel,
let no drop spill
between dark and dark
as I sing to skylark and sun
lifting up what I hold
to the light.

AFTER ECCLESIASTES

The day of death is better than the day of one's birth.

And the end of a party is better than the beginning.
Quietness gathers the voices and laughter
into one cup –
we drink peace.

Crumpled cushions are smoothed as our souls
and silence comes into the room
like a stranger bearing gifts
we had not imagined,
could not have known
without such comings
and such departures.

WORDS

I

Skimming, bruising, overloading,
diverting the traffic of signs,
words, weighty as stones,
crack the plank across the river
by which I try to reach you.

II

Out of the blue, words
are winged, migratory,
not staying
for answer, passing
overhead,
leaving, perhaps, an edge of song
to be filled in, sounded
through the silent winter pauses.

III

There are no words for this,
no nets to catch the leap from eye to eye,
no camera to keep
the haloed instant for eternity.

BOLTON-LE-MOORS, 1960

From Vernon Street in Bolton
you can lift your eyes up to the moors
forgetting traffic, grimed infirmary
and the Blind School where they weave baskets
in compensation.
Between mills' open fingers
you can see them
tawny as sleeping mastiffs
stretched out in the sun.
And Breightmet, rashed with bungalows,
is magical in mist
that kindly scarves a see-through school
with evening amethyst.
Never before in industry's complex
have I felt heather
and wind in the grasses –
the wild and the worked-on working together,
spinning the music of mills
from earth's resources.

THE BETTERWEAR MAN

The Betterwear man
stands at the backdoor and knocks
but I will not let him in.
On the doorstep he opens his case, displays
brushes, stain-removers, pan-scrubs
to scour my soul – my soul *is* scoured
by that gentle voice:
'This cleans cleaner than clean, removes
stains from inside the cup.'

I never feel dingier
than when I say No
to the Betterwear Man –
his goods are so good,
better than best,
lasting longer than life.

He's no right to pester me
with persuasion, promises, free-gifts –
today a needle-threader
till I'm drawn through myself –
but most of all, pity
that plugs me with guilt.
He pleads as with a daughter,
and I shut the door in his face.

Now he's gone I'm all wrung out
like a dish-cloth of not-clean water.

THE MILL CLOCK

The day he brought that old clock from the mill
and nailed it to the wall
he nailed his life there.
Morning and evening checked its time, Sundays
climbed on a chair to wind it,
set the pendulum
tick-tocking with his heartbeat.

On holidays he fretted, couldn't sleep
for listening to its silence,
came home early to wind it,
set it by the radio,
tilted it one degree as a careful mother
adjusts a pram to the wind,
folded a newspaper like a nappie
to stuff behind.
Sometimes it would go for half-an-hour;
once it ticked all day –
that night he slept like a child.
Next morning, silence.

After they took the clock away
he sat alone
jingling its rusty nails as he gazed
at the white space, the face of death
on the wall
ever with him, pacing round the house
losing things, forgetting things, but mostly
forgetting the time.

LOVE'S ADVOCATE

I remember sitting together in parks
leaning over bridges
counting trout and swans
holding hands under arches
kissing away suns
and moons into darkness.

I remember platform good-byes
last-minute trains
slamming us apart
and my non-self walking back alone.
I remember smaller things:
a pebble in my shoe
and you throwing a match-box on the Serpentine.

I stood still hearing the years
flow over and over
as over a stone
in a river-bed
polishing, cleaning, wearing away.
But I still remember the last day.

What I cannot remember is how I felt –
mind, love's advocate,
must remind heart
of the end, the abyss.
The bottom of the world remains;
each day climbs to a new start.

MY FAITHFUL LOVER

Though only his shadow
stalks me, I know
he is in the next room
waiting,
walking a black velvet world
without miles.

The calendar stares from the wall
blank as my diary,
but I know he will come –
not at my time or call –
so I run like a boy with a net
catching the sun
with every butterfly.

CLOWN

He was safe
behind the whitened face
and red nose of his trade,
vocation more certain
than doctor's or priest's
to cheer and heal.
Hidden away from himself
he could always make us laugh
turning troubles like jackets
inside out, wearing
our rents and patches.
Tripping up in trousers too long
he made us feel tall;
and when we watched him
cutting himself down,
missing the ball,
we knew we could cope.

What we never knew
was the tightrope he walked
when the laughter had died.
Nowhere to hide in the empty night,
no one to catch his fall.

SNOW LEOPARD

All things compose him –
atoms unresting,
snow-crystals, blood of earth and leaves.
Moon and sun
burn in his eyes. He breathes
rare mountain air; is silent
as a cloud above the flood
white-running over rock.

Printing the snow, his mark
affirms a presence that eludes –
beckoning while it holds at bay
to see beyond the mountains this
wild creature woven of myth before
knowledge and suffering
gripped us in the valley.

CLOWN FLOWERS

Three astonished sunflowers
gaze at me over the wall,
frilled faces saucer-eyed
at being giraffe-tall.

Clown flowers,
cariacatures; grist
to humorist and advertiser,
emblems
for Sun Life Insurance,
life-blood of Flora
in pure margarine
polyunsaturated.

PAINT BOX

He tried to tell them what he felt,
could say it only in colours –
Sunday's white page shading to grey
of evening clocks and bells-in-the-rain.
Monday morning, bright yellow brass
of a cock crowing.
Story-time, purple.
Scarlet is shouting in the playground.

His world's a cocoon
round as an egg, an acorn
sprouting green.
The schoolroom square and hard;
his desk hard and square
facing the enemy blackboard.

'You must learn to read,' they said
and gave him a painting-book alphabet.
Apple swelled beautifully red. Balloon
expanded in blue.
C was a cage for a bird;
his brush wavered through
painting himself
a small brown smudge inside.

LIMBO

Flung with door-slam and whistle-blow
into this carriage
I'm a snapshot torn
between two faces,
torn through myself
who yesterday in the garden
weeded and tended, mother among flowers,
asking only the quiet house,
long evening silences, and slow
peace of sunsets.

Now I'm in strange country –
fields, farms, steeples hurtle by
relentless in rhythm.
A woman talks to my incompleteness.
Is she, too, driven
by this terrible engine?
Rhythm, rhythm, railway, river
running voice accompaniment
to emptiness.
Sky and self all hollow.
I am outside, locked out from return.
No house will open to a wanderer
who's lost the key.

REPLY TO A PHILISTINE

Not even if you went on hands and knees,
read all the books,
put yourself through hoops,
could you enter this dimension.
Your sight is down the barrel of a gun.

It's not a matter of getting there,
of endeavour and desire,
but of knowing the unmapped country.

To see this you bring field-glasses
and a compass.
There's no
microscope can show you
that primrose by the river's brim
as something more.

A CHILD'S GUIDE TO PHILOSOPHY

Things as they are
are as they are because
they aren't
otherwise, said Kant.

Before him Aristotle,
thinking about thinking,
drew a cork from a bottle
to find the world altered by drinking.

Descartes thought
and said *Sum*.
Hobbes found life nasty
and short.

Schopenhauer would rather
have never been born –
it was he should have poured
the hemlock and drunk it.
But Kierkegaard,
though crippled, deplored
lack of faith for the leap
in the dark –
he himself wouldn't funk it.

Bentham found goodness in pleasure;
Mill disagreed.
How can we draw up a creed
with such contradictions
in efforts to know what cannot be known?
From Wittgenstein's answer –
'Get rid of the question'?

SCAPEGOAT

The ancients – all males, of course –
wrote the story in reverse.
The Tale of the Rib,
woven from pride and guilt,
is irrelevant.
It all began with Eve
lying alone in the grass
enjoying the apple
he hadn't the wit to discover.
Politely she handed it
to him who bit it greedily
undoing her
with his lost innocence.

Adam, the betrayer,
hearing his name
pouring down in accusation,
put up his umbrella
covering himself,
leaving Eve in the rain.

THE JOKE

'Explain the joke,' he said
adjusting his hearing aid.
So I picked a daisy,
plucked out the petals one by one,
used eyebrow tweezers for the florets,
entered the count of both,
along with the sepals,
in a red notebook – A, B, C.
'Now,' I said, handing it to him,
'put on your reading glasses.'
'But it's only figures and facts,' he objected,
'which tell me nothing.
And you've spoilt the daisy.'
'That's the joke,' I said.

ACADEMIC

He collected facts
as a pigeon picking up corn,
but his terrain, the library,
produced only husks
around life's grain.

From these he wove a garment
of knowledge – though threadbare within
he knew all the answers.

What he did not know
was the living tongue
in his listeners
whose questions he silenced
with deadly certainty.

RETREAT

The mountain above them rose
impenetrable, terrifying,
not with rock ledges, chasms,
but with the void.
Footsteps muffled in snow; voices
vanished on the wind; here
was power, passive, silent,
reducing rebellion to a nursery game.

No retreat from nothing;
overwhelmed by echoes
of what they could not know,
they looked at one another
speechless, diminished.
Then one smiled, remembering
his transistor.

EMILY DICKINSON

Others wore colours; I wore white
for one who never came –
whose coming was his going that
left me here alone.
I'll not expect a knocking on
my name carved in stone.

MOVING STAIRCASE

Living in the present is
surviving
in quicksand, keeping
the chosen level
on a moving staircase.

Try holding the sun
from setting
or promised fruit
in the moment of grasping
that slips through your netting
on to darkening grass.

Into the night
all tangibles pass;
of has been and is
only the imprint
remains.

THE PARTY

The best party of all is when,
The host being absent, the guests –
relations, friends, and neighbours – gather
to drink his health now he's taken
the final cure.

Praises sung, they relapse
into themselves, rejoicing
in this bringing together
by one whose going resolves
frictions in the estranged,
the half-remembered, half-forgotten,
all changed,
who wish him the happiest birthday
with no returns.

AUTUMN AT WHITEWELL

I stand upon dry leaves;
others come spinning down
while trodden memories
rustle through my brain
vague as river sound
lulling the afternoon.

Now prickling rain
scratches through sense to thought:
I see why autumn fills
more than woods and roads
with lifetime flower and fall
pressing the colours close,
packing promise lost and tall
in smallest range.

Strange that experience
grown out of hand and brain
should drop back leaf by leaf
each vein
a scrawled reminder...
A robin threads his song between
needles of larch and rain.

ROOTS

Even a tree has inclination
leaning
to east or west,
north or south
which we, sophisticated
with layer minds, prejudices,
preconceptions,
would label left and right,
rich and poor, unseeing
through the impartial swing of the wind
in the seed's setting,
the root and branch propulsion
of a tree's integrity.

We, who grow through choices
regarding the tree
as swayed beyond itself,
passive, obedient to changing winds,
commanding voices,
have lost direction in the breakaway
of mind
to power beyond capacity to hold
from roots that bind.

SUN UP

Apollo, Christ and God, all three
met in the first sunrise.
God's hand before Apollo's eyes
shadowed the land with the first tree,
and the man behind the sun came down
and walked upon the sea.

'We are the Light of the World,' said Christ
and Apollo in unison –
fire and flesh of the hidden spark.
'And I', said God, 'am the Three-in-One
who struck the match in the dark.'

HOW TO DO IT

How do the birds do it?
You hear them singing
fit to turn the leaves
and swell the bushes.

See them weaving –
flashing shuttles in-and-out the branches.
But you never see them dying
or even dead.

How do they do it
so tidily there's never a feather
to sweep up from the lawn –
unless the cat's around?

If only we
could emulate the birds and disappear
singing
out of sight and sound.

PARTRIDGE

She was round and warm and brown,
homely and soft as a fresh cob loaf.
She nestled you to comfort
from stings of nettles, thistles,
and wasp-thin tongues.
One could feel her
feathering her eggs, folding them
under her breast,
shuffling her wings
till all were safely gathered.

Her warmth of welcome shone
across a field;
you came to her out of the rain;
the wind lay down when she was near.
Sorrow that dropped from you
was dried, and laughter shook
easily as ears of corn.

I never heard her sing;
her song was herself.

THE CAP

After three days dragging
They found him, mouth in the mud, hair
Tangled with weeds and roots of water-lilies;
And here and there about him
Whose careful fly – Dark Snipe and Purple –
Had hovered temptingly,
A trout nosed, curious.

Now was the mayfly season
Which year by year
Had found him standing stiller than a heron
Among the reeds. Patient as a heron while he cast
Again, again above the ruffled water.

He was the archetype of fishermen,
Native to the brown-green silences
Of trout-pool, lake, and river,
Unborn into the world of chattering boxes,
Flickering screens outside his ring of leaves
That greeted his return
Until the day of no return.

Only a gentleman, the searchers said,
Wondering at the order of his going,
Would first take off his cap
And leave it for our guidance on the wall.

JULY 2ND, 1916

'British Attack on The Somme'

Six o'clock reveille: Scamblers Farm
and a shotgun bolt withdrawn.
Thump on the trestle, the first pig is landed
twisting, screaming; overhead
fantails murmur soft as down
while these, necklaced fine and red
under the accurate knife,
are bubbling, gargling gouts of blood
congealing to rubies
on glistening cobbles and boots.

On my seventh birthday, torn
from a feathered dream, I awake
to nightmare loud and warm
trampling the summer air,
and I'm running, head down, through the gate
shielded by trees to the river.

UNICORN

On the fifth day
the unicorn
must have slipped God's mind
somewhere between horse and goat,
and so was made safe
from man and extinction.
But maybe that
was the primal intention?

Ever seeking a gentle lady
beside whom to lie down,
he travels the world
unguided, invisible.
Archetypal, he faces
the lion beneath the crown.

Beyond this painted emblem
he wanders still,
a shadow seeking the light
in that patient woman who waited
through the dark night of nails
and thorn on the hill.

ORPHEUS IN THE UNDERGROUND

In the moment of looking back
From the top step
Of the escalator
The white flower of her face
Tilted towards him
Melted into the crowd.
And the tunnel sucked her underground.

The crowd surged upward
Pushing him into
The concrete world,
Mirrors mocked him; voices
Demanded rock for dancing;
Stamping feet stamped on
The hems of grief; breaking
His guitar strings; hands
Unstrung him, flung him
Singing into the Thames.

PROTEAN LOVER

I have a lover, but he's made of paper;
I read him back through words unwritten, find
A stranger hidden in the space between
Lines that lead me dancing, leave me blind.

I have a lover, but he's made of glass;
I see straight through him till I only see
My searching eyes reflected and reflecting
Receding images of him in me.

I have a lover, but he's made of water;
Lost to myself I plunge and swim alone
Away from the crumbling shore, compelled by the current
To drink the life I seek until I drown.

TRUTH GAME

He's peeled another skin
off my onion,
and I feel the cold, exposed
naked to truth, as to a knife.
In such undress is no redress – a cut,
because onions cannot bleed,
draws no blood, but peeling
such as his that makes no mark,
allows no healing.

SURVIVAL

Survival is the Word
Uttered in the egg –
Blackbird swallows silent worm
And turns it into song:
Usurping cuckoo pushes the young
Out of a song-bird's nest.
And where's the foetus needing air
That would not kill its host?

But aphids, labelled double X,
Must have the edge on us –
Virgins all, they reproduce
By parthogenesis.
Aphids eating rosebuds
Are food for ladybirds
Whose scarlet armour is no guard
Against a hungry wren.
Thus united hand-in-glove
With death, life munches on.

STARLINGS

Starlings have good ears:
they pick up threads of song
from blackbirds, thrushes to deceive us
with variations from chimney-pots.

Starlings fool us
with originality,
cuckooing the lover
with spring rhapsodies,
luring schoolboys out of school.

Starlings are found in libraries,
pecking among bookshops,
nesting a season in museums.
Adept at worming in dictionaries,
darting through leaves
of encyclopaedias, this breed,
crop-full of knowledge,
is practised in the art
of eclectic harvesting
whose corn serves to gloss
their borrowed plumes.

BRAIN CHILD

They sit up late
weighing synonyms,
twisting syntax to outwit understanding.
Phrases are scalpelled
in deliberate surgery.

Come dawn, the seed
dug up from the dark bed of unknowing,
is dissected;
labour's brain child analysed,
fragmented, cannot flower.

THE SHAPING SPIRIT

As a woman selecting threads
From a swatch of colours,
He selects words
Of many shades, tones, nuances.
Each to be weighed, measured,
Tongue-tested, and applied
According to relevance, shaped
Into stanzas, and what then
But a conglomerate
Of words unfired as a lump of clay
Without the shaping spirit?
Not to be teased into life
By will or desire,
But by giving air and space
To that which, seasoned as wood,
Catches fire.

NO REPLY AT CHRISTMAS

I have called you many times;
it's always No Reply.
And the answer from Enquiries
is my own question –
'What town and name?'
when the name's not in the book.

In the dark I go out, walking
through the Christmas wood
where the star that stood over a stable
is under a cloud.

When I ask its position
in the heavens, they laugh deriding
faith in an old story
woven of myth and fairy-tale,
and leave me in the cold
wind blowing away even rags
of comfort.

But I cannot go back –
my footprints are filled with snow,
the track obliterated.
And I cannot go on through the blind
night. I will forget time and the winter,
and wait, not seeing
but hoping.

A JOLLY GOOD FELLOW

For he's a jolly good fellow
And so say all of us.

And who's this jolly good fellow
Who joins in song and dance
And leads us in the chorus, why
It's Jesus!

Come, bring your ukelele
Or maybe a guitar
And play it at the altar;
He likes it better far

Than solemn organ music
And grey repeated chants –
We blow the Master's trumpet
In multi-coloured pants.

Fill up the bath with water
And plunge the baby in
And name it one of us who come
To wash away our sin.

We drink him in Ribena
And eat him in brown bread;
We rock-an'-roll to heaven
And clap our hands instead

Of being still and silent
Before a Mystery:
It is an open secret
Divulged to you and me –
The man is dancing with us
Who died upon a tree.

You can tell the same old story,
Give it another name
But he *is* a jolly good fellow
Just the same.

RETURN

I was always away from myself,
a shadow opening
doors without rooms, falling
short of being,
nobody's ghost, seeing
unseen,
a stranger meeting
me face to face in the dark.

Now all the rooms and beds are mine;
I am mistress of the switches.
Darkness rocks me, day
breaks into poetry and music.
No one locks me out of the inner room.

If the house feels empty
I think of those
whose absence has made me someone
I could never have known.

VISION

Here at the gate where understanding ends
Vision begins, for only silence calls
Louder than any voice, and darkness bends
My stubborn will to truth.
I cannot see the way and yet I pass
Beyond the measured boundaries of mind.
Shine on me as the sun on window-glass
Till I transmit the light I cannot find.

EDWARD THOMAS

Out of the woods he came;
From some green world his other life began
In way-back bondage to a god half man,
Half goat who knew each bird and leaf by name.

Often the stars he wondered at went blind
As he unseeing struggled in the dark,
Brick-walled captive of a searching mind,
Lost to his loved ones, trampling the spark
He lived by in the mud.

Through this quick anger poisoning the blood
There comes a bead of song, a thread of sound
Lifting the choking gloom; he wakes to see
The first primrose, a wood anemone
Whiter than milk from winter underground.

And the world is light, light as the first day;
Creation holds him singing in its power,
Perceiving truth in beauty hidden away
In a wren's egg, rain, and dust on a nettle flower.

MASTER COTTON SPINNER

Bolton, Lancashire, in the 1950s

The mill's black finger
Thrusting higher through the mist
Than the steeple of St Peter,
Has pointed his childhood to work,
Money, and power at the top,
Shadowed each working hour,
Bricked-in his dreams,
Written his will in a smoke-plume.

Overalled at seventeen,
He trod his father's mill barefoot
On hot, greased boards,
Serving the mules,
Nursing the thread
Into white cocoons, fattened
Upon whirling spindles
In damp heat tasting of oil,
Noise dimming speech to lip-language
As he learned the cool feel
Of cotton ripened by Egyptian sun.

Grading each load, was himself upgraded
To foreman, manager; he remained
Servant of machines, friend of spinners,
Bob, Jim, and Fred in the warm club
Fumed with beer and tobacco,
Refuge and home where differences were levelled
On the same floor.

He played bowls for Hawkshaw's,
Visited them in hospital –
Spinners' cancer fruiting in their vitals
Was reckoned a voluntary, while he
Sat uneasy in his office chair.

Red sky at morning: the spinners' warning;
The rising sun, crimson,
Soundless, sounded a gong
With cheap, bright frocks from Japan,
Gaudy towels from Pakistan
To dazzle in chain-stores.

It was short time for them.
The mill closed one day a week,
And then two.
Idle machines rusted, were scrapped.
His new job was scrapping the older men.
Evenings found him empty, threadbare,
A blind drawn down his face.

Still the colourful bales flowed in
Easy as eastern flowers, cajoling
Buyers to ignore snags in the cloth.

Through silence of spindles and looms,
Queues at the labour exchange,
And rents unpaid, still the flood,
Ominous as the Styx,
Gulped and rose outside the gates.

Seven hours
Round a boardroom table reduced it
To a trickle in the Take Over.
Hawkshaw's brick-built name written
Over a century's endeavour,
Survived on paper – in small print.

New managers were enlisted,
Young men roped against disaster
In competition's tug-of-war.
The last of the old comrades –
Deadwood Jim and Fred, were his for the cutting.

He was a job for the chairman
Who shook his hand, presenting him
With a gold watch and chain.

Unmanned, redundant, unnamed in the crowd,
He watched Hawkshaw's chimney felled like a tree.
But a tree falls whole, stretched proud to its highest leaf;
The doomed chimney collapsed like a toy
Into smoking rubble;
You could hear a sparrow fall
In brick-dust of that choking silence.

He returns daily to tread the mill
In the supermarket risen in its stead,
Fingering tins as he fingered the spindles,
Pulling the years' thread from his ravelled sleeve.

IMPRINT

It is a footprint
In sand or snow
With nobody there.

It is a voice.
But when I question, I hear
Only the wind
Fingering dead oak leaves,
Lifting
The stiffened fir tree branches.

It is the form
Of a hare – grasses
Still warm
And rounded from its resting,
But empty as air.

It is nothing and no one
Who can be known,
Only the imprint
Of somebody there.

ALL HALLOWS

(for Hilbre)

Walking among the antlered oaks,
Beeches, birches going gold,
Bracken, fox and squirrel-red,
I walk with ghosts.

It's not the sorrow of being old
But simple grief to be the last
Which overlays these coloured joys
With none to share the memoried past
Time only half destroys.

I wait until the ripe sun sets
And watch the trees,
How they count the days with leaves
And no regrets.

SUNDOWNER

In the last light of a late
October day
Let me go like a flake
Of whitening ash as I slowly burn
Down from the sun towards the day's return.

A POEM IS A PAINTING

A poem is a painting that is not seen;
A painting is a poem that is not heard.

That's what poetry is –
a painting in the mind.
Without palette and brush
it mixes words into images.
The mind's edge sharpens the knife
slashing the canvas with savage rocks,
twisting trees and limbs into tortuous shapes
as Van Gogh did,
or bewitched by movement's grace,
captures the opalescent skirts
of Degas' ballet dancers.

But words on the page
as paint on canvas
are fixed.
It's in the spaces between
the poem is quickened.

SURVIVORS

As wanton boys, we kill them for our sport
And our survival; where'd we be
Without the teasing fly, the pricking flea
To vent our wrath upon?

No need to dress up in red coats
Or carry guns; the primal joy
In killing's here at home:
Window-frame a battlefield,
Left-out meat, innocent fruit, a pot
Of honey – traps for satisfaction.

No guilt in this enjoyment; lust
grown savage speeds the spray, though best
Of all the lethal crack
Of thwacking magazine
That lays them flat
Who one day may arise
Survivors
Immune to all the gods' devices.

NAKED OSTRICH

People meeting at parties
or tête-a-tête across desk or table,
are of the same species –
the naked ostrich.
Talk of politics, the arts, the weather,
we're in daylight country,
mention death, and a blind comes down:
they shrink and silence grows.
Switch to gardens, wild life, travel,
and we're above ground again.

I find myself alone;
no coat in the wind –
the subject can be changed, but not the wind.
'Why must you ask?' they say,
'what cannot be answered?'
They are wise;
contentment lies deep, unstirred.
Out in the wind are no replies,
only echoes of Pilate's question.

ANIMALS' LAST WORDS

'I'm dyed, not dead,'
The ostrich said
Pluming from a prince's head.
'Save my bacon!' squealed the pig,
The sheep: 'Keep off my rug!'
The thieving jack hare chased too often
Shrieked: 'I'm in the jug!'
'Lucky you,' the turtle gurgled,
'I am in the soup!'

The soup, the soup, the meaty meeting-
place of many of us –
Horse and hound and hartebeest
And hippopotamus.

'Cheer up do,' the pigeon coos,
'We all of us must die.
Hot from heaven comes my news –
It's warmer in the pie!'
But Bill, the black bull, bellows:
'MY EYE!'

CHANGING COLOUR

It happened slowly
as a cygnet turns from grey to white,
but in Saville Street it happened in reverse –
from white to ivory to café-au-lait
to strong black coffee,
and from drab to bright –
greys and duns to ruby, turquoise, emerald,
from brass to reed –
reed music quickening soft, sandalled feet
hushing the tapping pavements
in rhythm of a dance,
strange tongues and voices at front doors
confusing us.

Now we've learned the tune
in bangles, saris, turbans,
flashing jewels
from molten sand and stone –
hot jungle music
vibrating through the northern rain.

COMPARISON WITH A SUNFLOWER

Seeded, brown beyond admiration,
The sunflower, having passed its prime,
Expects no responses from the sun.
I, too, like the sunflower,
Demanding nothing, am liberated,
Free from erratic seasons of the heart,
Am suspended, wingless, between
Pendulum swings tick-tocking away
The emptiness of age when, for me,
Unlike the sunflower, mindless on its stalk,
Awareness sharpens with the shortening days.

SO LITTLE IT CAN TAKE

One leaf on a line
cannot delay a train,
but many fallen together
heaped, and damped by rain
can halt the screaming express,
disrupt appointments, prevent
meetings and bonds of love.
A sideways move can shake
dice from a ladder's foot
to the head of a snake.
So little it can take
to change design to disorder,
man into bone
as, with time, a drop of water
can change the face of a stone.

AFTER VERLAINE

It snows in my soul
As it snows on the ground
And the cold in my soul
Is the cold in the sound
Of a snow-laden wind
From a maiden-white cloud.

Very fine are the flakes
Very soft is the fall
Mother-soft fingers
Are weaving a shawl,
Are folding a shawl
Until the thread breaks.

WALKING BACK

Walking again along these well-loved paths
misted with bluebells,
between translucent beeches, young in leaf,
and strong horse-chestnuts
holding up white candles to the day,
is a kind of bereavement.

Family and friends departed,
and many dead,
every cottage altered by new owners,
and the white house where we lived
painted, smartened, tastefully modernised.
It was a Georgian rectory where
Jane Austen might have lived –
a little shabby, threadbare,
yet breathing history, a home for poets
more than novelists, it was
a Walter-de-la-Marish sort of house.
Shadowed branches in the moonlight
laced the walls mysteriously.
Often an owl called from the poplar tree
slim as a mast, the tree where one star,
like a bird, lodged in the topmost branches.

I used to stand against the garden wall
looking up to the house I loved and vowed
never to leave.
The marguerites in front were little moons
silver, silent, in the mothy night.
Now all is changed – the younger son went first,
and then the father. All the rest have followed.
One by one they went, but I must stay
returning sometimes, foolishly, to recall
memories better left
sleeping among the fells, under the trees,
and withering with these bluebells. Strange
how one can bury all but these!

THE RIVALS

They gave them royal names
Those rousing stallions –
Blackthorn Blueblood
Redstone King –
Black and bay
Flagging the lanes with ribbons and rosettes,
Fetlock-feathered, flinging their way
Across windy yards.

Manes straw-plaited
Prided with bells and flowers,
These two were rivals –
Redstone's pedigree
Was starred with champions
But Blueblood's owner charged the higher fee.

Farmers prized a foal
By the giant black
Satin-shining, smooth as coal,
Prick-eared, buckling on delight.
Yet sometimes fumbling the bolt
He failed to slam it home.
While Redstone, sure, compact
Covered his mares with ease
Indifferent to the certain gift
Delivered quietly as a fall of snow.

THE GYMNASTS

All at once I saw them
whirling arms and legs – the gymnasts
doing handstands on the high fell
linking past and future.
Here are the four winds caught
bridled and harnessed to our use.
Could Caratacos in his wild rides
have seen them! Now it seems
plans from another planet in our hands
are witnessed on Cold Clough Moor.
Tall and slim and white
twirling the air, they offer warmth and light
to thirty thousand living there below
in the rugged valley feathered with rowan and birch.
For them, no power-cuts or strikes
only the wind's variations.
But my first sight of the twenty-four
racing, while rooted, in unison
was wonder and delight electrified.

FROM WALDEN

Thoreau's House in the Woods

'Three chairs –
one for solitude, two for company,
three for society,'
a bed, a table, what more
for a wish?
Or for warmth, a wood fire?

Worlds of spring and summer
stream through my windows.
Time and space for thought: I dwell
without stairs on many levels,
fired by unanswered questions –
how comes the clam, thick-shelled
sunk deep in river mud
by its rainbow colours?
Or the celandine its shine
even without the sun?

I have east and west in my windows;
the door opens south
inviting me out, shutting me
against rain.
I need no ornaments, having all outside.
I sit among grasses
that gather no dust, am rich
with earth's coinage
that spills and is ever replenished.

Which way I go in the woods
I follow the Indian's track:
first come, he is wise
reading the wind, and the moon's seasons.
By the moon, not the sun,
his days are measured,
and by winters his life.

Lights, dazzling-bright,
he leaves to the white man
whose power will eat away forests
and flatten the earth.
Everywhere
the white man set his foot
the land is sore.
While the Indian inhabits Nature,
the white man invades.
In darkness and silence
the Indian finds his way
through brushwood and pine,
even the blue jay
is quiet at his coming; the owl
salutes him.

Thoreau Speaks from Walden

Sitting alone in my cabin
watching the woodchucks play
and the striped racoons
streaking through the shadows,
I know I have much to learn from the Indian
who is free
while the minister confines himself
in words and argument.

Civilized man will rule the world
outside himself, forgetting
what the Indian has not lost
and both were given,
for both have been children.

Civilization!
What have you done that so many
live lives of quiet desperation?
I'll return to my three chairs
with Alcott and Emerson;
we'll talk the night into sunrise
till we find there's a way through the forest
without destroying the trees.

DAYS

Days, like sand, run through the hour-glass,
Flash by on the ticker-tape,
Turn the summer into winter,
Change the shape
Of facts and faces, rub out names
Cut with passion into tree-trunks,
Type out other ones instead,
Moss-fingered, fill the letters written
In stone to tell us who is dead,
Unweave the plover's nest in passing –
Days are egg-shells where I tread.

DEFEATHERED

Unlocking the bathroom;
handing over the keys of the house;
exposing privacies
while hiding the soul, invaded
by helpers, yet needing their help,
resenting
the necessity of pity;
accepting, receiving, thanking
without giving, being
wrong side of the door, pretending
to be happy free from pain while knowing
the peacock's treasured tail
defeathered,
is to act out 'the last stage of all'
as though
the curtain were not about to fall.

FROM THE DAY ROOM

The people here are not here.
Where are they gone who have left themselves behind?
Why does this one pluck her skirt all day?
And why, this Monday morning,
does the grey man, stuffed in a wheelchair,
not read the *Sunday Times*
propped up before him?

From the day room a lake
glitters before us; snowdrops
whiten and shake in the grass, and squirrels
raise question-mark tails,
aptly inverted for questions
that cannot be answered.

Perhaps I
am saddest of all who feel the Spring
groping around us, and the call
in the air inviting us on
into the sun and a world
of rising sap and renewal.

THE LEAVE TRAIN

The train is moving;
Out of the window I'm waving;
Sister, daughter, friend, and son
Wait on the platform unaware
The train has gone.

Behind them, relations, people
At parties, in shops, in the street –
People I know by sight but not to meet:
They cannot see
The light gone green for me
On a line untravelled.
One day they, one at a time,
Will take the train,
Each to a different destination
Not yet printed in the guide.
Yet every ticket's ordered in advance.

Under the clock they hurry
Home and back again
Making a dance of the time-table, believing
The train they must catch
Is not yet running.